That One Thing

A search for significance

JUSTYN REES

www.justynrees.com
justynrees@gmail.com

BIG TREE PUBLISHING
LANGLEY, BC

Published by Big Tree Publishing
Langley, BC Canada
ISBN 978-1-9992463-0-3

www.justynrees.com
justynrees@gmail.com

That One Thing © 2019 Justyn Rees
All Rights Reserved, except where otherwise noted

Do you know what the secret of life is?... Just one thing.
You stick to that and the rest don't mean shit.
Curly in City Slickers

Love and be loved! That is the only reality in the world,
all else is folly. It is the one thing we are interested in here.
War and Peace, Leo Tolstoy.

One thing I ask of the LORD. This is what I seek.
Psalm 27:4, *The Bible*

JUSTYN REES

A storyteller and writer, Justyn is passionately concerned for peace and reconciliation in a broken world. Amongst his many adventures he journeyed for five years with a mobile theatre company from town to town across Canada presenting the story of reconciliation at a time when national division seemed inevitable. Following the genocide in Rwanda, he led a forty strong delegation from Canada and the UK appealing for forgiveness to a people divided by racial and religious atrocities. He regularly lectures in war-weary Ukraine inspiring teachers to pass on the gift of love and forgiveness to a coming generation. Justyn has written several books, including *To Make an Old Story New* and *To Make a Long Story Short*.

Love

My dad loved my mum, and voila! Me.

But it didn't start there. My two grandpas loved my two grannies, and before them my four great-grandpas loved my four great-grannies. Somewhere I have a dog-eared brown-and-white photo, taken soon after photography was invented, of my great-great-great-great-great-grandparents, who were born in the 1790s. I must have had 120 such great ancestors, each of whose love for the other contributed to me. Well, that's a lot of loving! But that's only recent history. How many cavemen loving the cavewoman down the canyon did it take to determine the exact seeds of who I now am? And I guess that wasn't even the beginning either. Billions of my amoeba grandpas must have loved billions of my amoeba grannies as they wiggled out of the primeval swamp. Without them each loving each other I wouldn't be the man I am today!

Or perhaps Darwin was wrong. Maybe there were no

amoebas or apes—just Adam and Eve. But even *their* love for each other was the germ of who I am.

The point is, I owe my life to love. Love is responsible for who I am. Love forged every single link in the chain of humanity from which I hang, and if I don't love someone else, I'm the final link. End of.

Love may not be all the world is made of, but it is an important ingredient. Us humans are at our best when we love, when we show kindness and gentleness. 'Humanity', we call it. But unkindness, violence and hate are also human qualities, and we don't insult ourselves by dubbing them 'humanity'.

Hate

So, what about hate? If love started the process, hate has always done its miserable best to end it. Three of my great-uncles were blown to oblivion in the trenches of World War I, but somehow my grandparents made it through unscathed. And my parents survived the Blitz of World War II in London. The delicate chain of love that led to me survived hate's ravages.

Back in the early days, the best tools that hate had at its disposal were swords and spears. But now guns and bombs have multiplied hate's potential to the point that one disgruntled person could annihilate the whole human race with one touch of the proverbial button. Love may make the world go round, but I fear that hate may knock it off its axis before long.

War and Peace! Perhaps Tolstoy was right when he said, 'Love and be loved! That is the only reality in the world, all else is folly.'

So where does hate come from? I fear that I'm as responsible as anyone for its existence, as capable of unkindness as the next man. If I can't make my home, my street, my neighbourhood, my town a more loving place to live, then I'm no help. Perhaps I'm even part of the problem.

Love Defined

The best definition of love I can find runs like this:

> *Love is patient, love is kind. It does not envy, it does not boast, it is not proud. It is not rude, it is not self-seeking, it is not easily angered, it keeps no record of wrongs. Love does not delight in evil but rejoices with the truth. It always protects, always trusts, always hopes, always perseveres. Love never fails.*

Who can argue with that, eh?

Someone to Love

There are over seven billion of us humans. You can't love them all, but love does need an object, a focus, right? I mean, you can't just love in a vacuum, all on your own. You have to have something or someone to love.

Love your neighbour. That's more like it. He's real. She lives next door.

Love God. Yes, but where does he live? And is he real?

People all over the world seem to share a certain vertical instinct that makes us want to reach up into the great void above our heads, something or someone supreme, someone to help us when we are in trouble, someone to thank when Thanksgiving Day rolls round, someone to blame when disaster strikes or the insurance company needs an excuse not to pay up, someone to guide us when the great GPS of life is on the fritz, someone to keep us company when there's no internet or TV, someone to copy when we need a superhero. *Someone to love.*

Instinct

Reaching towards God seems to be instinctive, as vital to our survival as breathing.

All my other instincts lead me to some fundamental necessity that is good for my health. Hunger leads me to food—got to eat. Thirst—can't go long without a drink, can we? Fatigue—eight hours of shuteye so I can face another day. Fear—must run from danger to preserve my precious little skin. Sex—well, now we're talking! Got to keep the population growing. And love? Yes!

But how about loving God? Is God real? And is he

good for me like the other objects my instincts urge me to reach for?

Mr. Google tells me that believing in God actually is good for my health: it reduces blood pressure, strengthens the immune system and improves mental health. People who believe in God live longer, happier lives. So, if God were just a delusion, I can't help but think that such self-deception should have a negative outcome, but no! Turns out God is good for me.

But is God true? Is he real, or just a placebo, an invention for the benefit of my health?

If every other instinct leads me to something real that I actually do need, it would be kind of odd to imagine that the instinct that leads me to reach for God is the only red herring on the beach. *Just kidding! No one home!*

The fact that my instinct reaches out for God, and that doing so enriches my health, suggests that perhaps God is a reality that I need, along with food, drink, sleep, sex and all the other goodies.

But there are some bizarre notions out there of what God is like—crude statues with multiple heads, arms and legs and gross appendages. So should I throw out the baby with the bathwater, reject God altogether because some folks have wacky ideas of what they imagine he's like?

But I suppose I shouldn't criticise other people's ideas. After all, everyone's entitled to their own opinion, right? So I turned to Mr. Google to ask what God is like…

Popular Choice

It's all a question of religion. Seems there are many brands out there, each with their own ideas about God. Christianity tops the world religion charts, with Islam a good second. But wasn't Christianity invented by conservative Americans, the Born Again crowd from down south?

No. Apparently not. Two thousand years ago, way back when Rome ruled the earth, Christianity was doing nicely, thank you. A couple of quotes caught my eye.

Cornelius Tacitus, a Roman senator, writing about the great fire of Rome in AD 64, said that Emperor Nero tried to divert attention from himself by blaming the disaster on the local Christians:

Nero fastened the guilt and inflicted the most exquisite tortures on a class hated for their abominations, called Christians. Christus, from whom the name had its origin, suffered the extreme penalty during the reign of Tiberius at the hands of one of our procurators, Pontius Pilatus.

But I can't help but wonder if what Christians were

doing back then bore any resemblance to what passes for Christianity today. Pliny, an imperial magistrate of Rome at the end of the first century AD, wrote a letter to Emperor Trajan reporting that:

> *The Christians were in the habit of meeting on a certain fixed day before it was light, when they sang a hymn to Christ, as to a god, and bound themselves by a solemn oath, not to do any wicked deeds, never to commit any fraud, theft or adultery, never to falsify their word, nor deny a trust after which it was their custom to partake of food of an ordinary and innocent kind.*

So there you are then. Two thousand years old and counting.

Books

Mr. Google kindly suggested a number of holy books I might like to consult on the subject of God.

The Bible tops the list, the world's all-time bestseller, translated into more than 2,800 languages. But even with such impressive stats on its side, I can't help but think that the Bible should hardly boast to be the last word on God. Perhaps not the last word, but maybe it might offer some useful *first words*. Good place to start. And anyway, I already have a copy. So I pulled mine from the shelf and blew the dust off.

First impressions?

Well, it's thick and black—not exactly eye-catching—but despite that, I gave it a read. It's a bit daunting at first glance, but then a pattern emerged. There are two main sections, Old and New Testaments, with 66 smaller divisions some of them with strange unpronounceable names.

Actually, it's not always easy to follow the plot since there's ancient history and then there are predictions of what is yet to happen. There are sections of good advice and proverbs relating to every subject known to man. There's a few boring pages itemising regulations on hygiene that nearly lost me. But then there's poetry—at least I think it's poetry. Doesn't poetry have to rhyme just to qualify? This doesn't, though I notice that alternate lines seem to complement each other. That's a kind of rhyme, isn't it?

The bottom line is that it's impressive, fascinating, full of great stories that kept me turning the pages, well most of them anyway. I have to admit that some parts were a bit of a yawn.

Myths

But is it true, or just a book of myths? Perhaps there's another holy book out there that's closer to the mark? But life's too short to spend it reading thousands of religious books—and much too short to get involved in religious arguments. I am content to start with the Bible since I already have a copy. Anyway, it's the popular choice, a global bestseller, and all those people can't be wrong, can they?

So, here's what strikes me…

For starters, it doesn't read like make-believe or sci-fi. Take this paragraph, for example, the opener of one of the many sections of the Bible, written by a guy called Luke who claims to be an eyewitness:

> *Having carefully investigated all of these accounts from the beginning, I have decided to write a careful summary for you, to reassure you of the truth of all you have heard.*

Well that doesn't sound like 'Once upon a time'.

But more than that, the Bible is full of good sense, not like the ramblings of an impostor. If someone made it all up just to lead us down the garden path, then it is some impressive garden path.

Maps

At the back of my version of the Bible I see some maps. Apparently the Bible is not set in Never Never Land, but in real cities and countries with real rivers running through them that are still on Google maps today. I flew to Amman in Jordan recently, and our route took us right over Israel. I watched on the monitor as it showed the little airplane that pinpointed our position flying over a map exactly like the one in my Bible.

Google tells me that some forty different authors contributed books and articles over the 1,500-year period that it took to complete the Bible. Most of those guys could never actually have met each other, since they lived hundreds of years apart and in different countries and wrote in multiple languages. So it's doubtful they ever sat round a table with a publishing editor to discuss content and structure. Yet the Bible reads like one book.

Obviously my version of the Bible is not the original written in the handwriting of Matthew, Mark, Luke and John and all the other unpronounceables. They have all been dust for hundreds of years. Mine is just a copy of a copy.

I can't help but wonder how much the story might have grown legs over the 3,000 years since the early pages were first written. When I was a kid, we used to play Chinese whispers, a game in which a secret was whispered round the circle, and the joke was to hear the final version after it had been distorted by a dozen whisperers. So is my Bible just a joke, or does it bear any resemblance to the original story?

I did a little research and here's what I discovered…

Copies

The first half of the Bible, the Old Testament, was first written over 3,000 years ago, but until recently the oldest copy still in existence was only a thousand years old, leaving 2,000 years since the first page was originally written for copyists to get the story fouled up.

But then the year after I was born a shepherd nosing around in a cave near the Dead Sea discovered a bunch of scrolls sealed in old clay pots. The scrolls turned out to be old, really old, two thousand years old in fact, and included several sections of the Old Testament. Now here's the thing… These newly discovered pages of the Old Testament were a thousand years older than anything we had before, a thousand years closer to when the original had been written, yet in the intervening thousand years nothing had changed. I went to have a look at the scrolls for myself while on a visit to Jerusalem. Sure boosts my confidence that my Bible is not much changed from what was being read one, two and probably even three thousand years ago. So much for the old Chinese whispers game!

John was a close friend of Jesus. He wrote his biography that eventually found its way into the second section of the Bible, the New Testament. John's original handwritten version may be dust, but a wee section of a copy of it made just fifty years after John had put his original pen to his original paper was discovered down in Egypt, and is now safely preserved at the University of Manchester in the UK. Apparently there are thousands of further fragments dating from the following years which when pieced together cover the whole New Testament.

I visited the British Library in London to have a look at the oldest complete version of the New Testament. It sits nonchalantly in a glass case in a corner close to the Beatles' 'Strawberry Fields Forever' in John Lennon's handwriting. To my amazement, the 1,700 year old New Testament still looks as clear and fresh as today's newspaper—, and a good deal more legible than Lennon's scrawl.

A former director of the British Museum is recorded to have said:

> *The last foundation for any doubt that the Scriptures have come down to us substantially as they were written has now been removed. Both the authenticity and the general integrity of the books of the New Testament may be regarded as finally established.*

So it would appear that I have firm grounds to be confident that the Bible I own today contains pretty much exactly what was written way back by those forty ancient authors. I can rest easy in the confidence that that my big black Bible is no 'True stories made up from the legendary past.'

Hard Evidence

OK. So much for the paperwork. But has anyone dug

up any hard evidence to support what the Bible says?

I read an article in *Time* magazine about Dr. Nelson Glueck, described there as 'the greatest modern authority on Israeli archeology'. The article reported him as saying:

> *No archeological discovery has ever controverted a Biblical reference. Scores of archeological findings have been made which confirm in clear outline or in exact detail historical statements in the Bible.*

My archeological experience reached its peak the day I dug up a gas line in my back yard, so who am I to question Dr. Glueck?

But here's a little detail I stumbled upon. The Bible records that a king names Hezekiah, who reigned in Jerusalem around 700 BC 'blocked the upper outlet of the Gihon spring, made a pool and a tunnel by which he channelled the water down to the west side of the City of David' (Jerusalem).

That tunnel is still there. I know because I walked through it a few years back. Archaeologists found some ancient lettering etched into the rock wall of the tunnel celebrating the occasion when the miners, who had started digging at opposite ends, finally met in the middle. So those engineers must have got their calculations right, just as the Bible must have got that detail right.

But what happened to the pool that the Bible says was associated with the tunnel?

I dislike confined spaces, so I was relieved to eventually emerge from that damp hole into the sunlight, back at ground level. But right in front of me was a barrier to prevent me from falling into a hole where some repair work was being done on a drainage pipe, with apologies from the city for disruption caused. Apparently, in the course of that repair, they had unearthed a series of steps leading down into what looked like a swimming pool. Archaeologists identified it as the long-lost pool, the pool of Siloam, dug at the behest of King Hezekiah in 700 BC, as faithfully recorded in the Old Testament. That pool, buried by the Romans when they sacked the city in AD 70, and dug up again by city workers in AD 2004 was the same location where Jesus healed a blind man, as recorded in the New Testament.

Graffiti

I have been to Israel a couple of times. On my first visit back in 1973, I visited the Galilee, where a team of archaeologists were busy excavating ruins of the ancient village of Capernaum on the northwest shore of Lake Galilee. The focus of their archaeological excitement on the cold, wet day of my visit was the hexagonal-shaped footings of a building, protected from the elements by sheets of corrugated iron.

Recently I paid a return visit and found that the corrugated iron had been replaced by a magnificent building. Apparently, the archaeologists had at first perceived it to be just another dwelling, a few small rooms clustered around an open courtyard, dating from the first century BC. Further investigations revealed that the use of the house had soon after been dramatically upgraded. For one thing, the pottery used by the residents had changed from regular cooking pots and bowls to large storage jars and oil lamps, suggesting that the house had graduated from being simply a private residence to being a space that could accommodate communal gatherings. And then they found the graffiti: small crosses, a boat, and messages scratched on the walls written in Greek and Hebrew, such as 'Lord Jesus Christ, help your servant' and 'Christ have mercy'. The original house had apparently been converted into some kind of a holy shrine. They surmised that this had likely been the home of Peter, a local fisherman who gets quite a lot of press in the New Testament. If they were right, then that was the same home in which the Bible says Jesus lodged during his years in Capernaum.

Real People

One of the villains named in the Bible is an Italian politician, Pontius Pilate. He was the man the Bible holds responsible for sentencing Jesus to death. Did

Pilate have a mailing address? Yes, as it happens. On the shore of the Mediterranean Sea still stand the ruins of a magnificent waterfront palace built by Herod the Great back in the days when Jesus was still a toddler. In AD 26, Pontius Pilate got a new job as Governor of Judea and needed a place to hang his shingle. He took a shine to the beautiful waterfront location of Herod's palace, so he rented the place. In 1961 an archaeologist excavating the site found a limestone block bearing the name of the resident: Pontius Pilate, Prefect of Judea, just as described in the Bible.

A few miles round the Mediterranean Sea the impressive ruins of the city of Corinth still are visible. Judging from the footings that trace their outlines in the grass, Corinth boasted some impressive infrastructure. So, Erastus, who held the prestigious position of Commissioner of Public Works of that fair city, would have been an important man. Among his other achievements, Erastus sponsored a section of fine stone pavement in the city centre and was honoured for his generous contribution by having his name carved into its surface: 'Erastus, Commissioner of Public Works, laid this pavement at his own expense.' The day I visited Corinth it had been raining, and a dog was taking a drink from the water trapped in the deeply embossed tribute to Erastus. The man is still performing public works!

It was around this time that a New Testament preacher named Paul came to town. Erastus must have attended his lectures, for it would appear he became a believer and thus merited a mention in a letter Paul wrote to some friends in Rome. That letter got itself included in the New Testament: 'Erastus, who is the city's Commissioner of Public Works, sends you his greetings.'

Time Capsule

While the New Testament was still being completed, far away in the Italian city of Pompeii was a household in the habit of sharing family prayers, their favorite prayer being 'The Lord's Prayer', a prayer recorded in the Bible that Jesus had first taught his followers not far from home in Capernaum. These Pompeiians liked the prayer so much that they wrote it on a wall of their home. Then, on 24 August 79 AD, whoosh! Mount Vesuvius blew her top. They were all buried in volcanic ash and the whole of Pompeii became a time capsule that lay unopened for the best part of two thousand years till archaeologists excavated the long buried city. And there was the Lord's Prayer, still on the wall, just like the New Testament spells it out.

Mosaic

Just a few miles down the road from Nazareth, Jesus' boyhood hometown, stands the high-security

Megiddo Prison. There in the summer of 2005, Ramil Razilo was serving a two-year sentence for traffic violations. He was one of fifty Palestinian prisoners tasked with excavating the area before the construction of a new cellblock. To his amazement, Razilo laid bare a patch of beautiful mosaic. He and his fellow inmates worked for months uncovering a magnificent mosaic floor. There outlined in mosaic chips were two fish and ancient Greek letters that identified the building as being 'dedicated to the memory of the Lord Jesus Christ'.

I suppose that multiple washroom walls boasting 'Kilroy was here' don't prove there ever was a Kilroy with a bladder problem, but I am encouraged by all these etchings on the walls and floors of time to believe that what is written in my Bible is no mere figment of someone's recent imagination.

Contemporaries

It strikes me that if the events in the Bible are true, it would seem reasonable that some of the people and happenings it records would also have caught the attention of other contemporary journalists and historians. And yes, there are dozens of letters and articles outside the Bible that tell the same story.

Thallus described an eclipse of the sun that *'pressed on the whole world a most fearful darkness' and a concurrent 'earthquake that rent the rocks, and threw down many places in Judea'*.

So the Bible's account of the execution of Jesus when *'the darkness came over the whole land from the sixth hour until the ninth, and the subsequent violent earthquake'* was no isolated imagining dreamt up by someone with a hangover.

Phlegon, a Greek writer born at the end of the first century, wrote that *'Jesus arose after death, and exhibited the marks of his punishment, and showed how his hands had been pierced by nails'*.

Titus Flavius Josephus, sponsored by Emperor Vespasian, wrote a history of the Jews for the benefit of Roman scholars. Josephus, who had been a young man when the ink of the New Testament was still wet, wrote:

> *About this time there lived Jesus, a wise man, if indeed one ought to call him a man. For he was one who performed surprising deeds and was a teacher of such people as accept the truth gladly. He won over many Jews and many of the Greeks. He was the Messiah. And when, upon the accusation of the principal men among us, Pilate had condemned him to a cross, those who had first come to love him did not cease. He appeared to them spending a third day restored to life, for the prophets of God had foretold these things and a thousand other marvels about him. And the tribe of the Christians, so called after him, has still to this day not disappeared.*

Benchmark

Somewhere buried in the vaults of Rome are perhaps the records of a census commissioned by Caesar Augustus around the year dot that included an entry for a baby boy born on the day of the census in an obscure village in Judea named Bethlehem. The name on the entry? Jesus.

Of course, such a find has never actually been made, but my point is that that obscure birth has become the benchmark around which history is measured: before and after, BC and AD. History measured around a myth? Get real!

The bottom line of all this history and archaeology is that I don't have to be a complete moron with my head stuck you know where to take the Bible seriously. If I want to read up on God, then the Bible is a credible place to start.

Blank Sheet of Paper

What do I imagine God is like? My own thoughts…

For starters I'd guess he'd have to be old… old enough to have set the clock ticking when time began.

And he'd be big… big enough to have made space, and that's quite a reach, yet he'd need an eye for detail, nanoparticles and such.

Smart? Goes without saying.

Strong? Clearly some heavy lifting must have been required.

Wealthy? He'd have to be comfortable, wouldn't he? I can't fathom why religious people are always begging for money to help God out since God must know where he buried all the gold.

What Does the Bible say God is Like?

Looks like I totally underestimated him.

I guessed he'd have to be old. But the Bible describes him as *everlasting*—time without beginning or end. That's older than just old.

And I had him pegged as merely big. But *infinite* is how the Bible measures him. That's space with no edges, bigger than big. But trying to wrap my brain around such things as everlasting and infinite makes my brain ache. I just can't fathom. Yet I can't be far wrong when I guess that he must be greater than I can imagine just to qualify for the job. Maybe that's what I find so fascinating about God. I love the ocean. I love the little bit I can see on the surface all the more because of the mystery of what is under the surface and over the horizon.

Of course, I like to think God is *good*. But the Bible takes it further… *Perfect. Holy.*

And I credited God with being strong, but the Bible rates him *almighty*.

Wealthy? Surely he must have got by before we humans came along to help him out with a few coins in the offering on a Sunday. But once again the Bible goes further than merely wealthy.

> *The God who made the world and everything in it is the Lord of heaven and earth and does not live in temples built by hands. And he is not served by human hands, as if he needed anything, because he himself gives all men life and breath and everything else.*

Well, exactly. Just like I expected. *Wealthy*.

And where does God live? What's his address if he doesn't need us to build him a temple, or a mosque or a church? One of those religious hotspots like Mecca or Jerusalem? Or how about Heaven? The Bible simply addresses him as '*I AM*'. That seems to capture the ever-present, always-everywhere idea. The Bible puts him closer than next door. *God is not far from any of us.. In him we live and move and have our being.*

Right here, right now.

New Dimensions

Well, so far so good, even if the Bible does go way beyond my inadequate expectations. At least I am headed in the right direction. But the Bible adds several dimensions I had never thought of, like *personal*.

When George Lucas wrote *Star Wars*, The Force was his concept of God. 'Higher Power' is the limit of what most of us can imagine. But I notice the pronouns the Bible uses are always personal—'he' rather than 'it'. The Bible's God has feelings, grief, anger, jealousy, compassion, joy. Apparently he even enjoys a good laugh from time to time. And the Bible tells us that when he was looking for a representative on Earth to reflect him, something to mirror him, he passed over such impressive candidates as mountains, sun, moon and stars. In fact, he didn't choose a thing at all, but settled on us humans—personal. 'Let us make man in our image.' So, if we are made in God's image, it would seem to follow that he must be somewhat like us—*personal*—only more so. I for one am not an *it*. I'm a *he*.

So, is God a man or a woman? I can't help but imagine him as an old man with a long white beard. Thanks, Michelangelo! But the Bible once again takes it a step beyond even Michelangelo's chauvinistic imagining.

> *God said, 'Let us make man in our image, in our likeness.' So God created man in his own image, in the image of God he created him; male and female he created them.*

Seems it took both sexes to reflect God's likeness. And it gets more mind-stretching.

The Royal 'We'

The Bible repeatedly stresses that God is *one*. So who is he talking to when he says, 'Let us make man in our image'? Who is us? The royal 'We' as per Queen Victoria?

The world is full of people with vastly differing ideas about God. We can't all be right, can we? I can't imagine there being a smorgasbord of gods out there presiding over different parts of creation, all vying for our vote at the religious polling stations. So I warm to the Bible's description of God as *one*. But I am foxed by the *us*.

And the farther I read into the Bible, the more confused I get. 'Us' seems to have three faces—sometimes the face of a Father, sometimes a Son and other times a Spirit. 'Trinity' is the technical term I've heard used by religious folks to explain the inexplicable, though I don't find that word in the Bible.

So back to Mr. Google for an explanation, and I find various ideas.

Water can be liquid, solid or vapour, but it's always H²O. But I don't see how that explains God being three yet one!

Perhaps it's just a question of perspective. I'm a father. I'm a son. I'm a husband. My kids call me 'Dad'. My Dad calls me 'Son'. My wife calls me all kinds of things when I'm late home for dinner. But when all is said and done, there is only one me. That makes some sense.

Perhaps the concept of family is closest to the mark. If it took both sexes, male and female, to reflect what God is like and if when those two come together as one they produce a third, that makes family a kind of trinity. Bingo! Two into one make three!

Sex

I suppose sex was bound to come into the conversation eventually! But surely God is down on sex, right? Dirty word.

But hold on a moment… The only detail the Bible specifically includes about our similarity to God is that we are men and women, male and female. That's sex, isn't it? Nothing about us being black or white, short or tall, smart or stupid. There's not even any mention of religion. Just gender stuff, with the kit that makes babies.

Us humans have been at it ever since the first naked man met the first naked woman in the park, as documented in the second chapter of the Bible. Seems it was love at first sight, and the two of them came together in a loving embrace, a union, a moment of symphonic harmony, one like God is one. I wonder how surprised they were when nine months later out popped a baby human. 'With the help of God I have made a man!' exclaimed the astonished woman when she'd stopped yelling, amazed at her own creativity.

'I wonder what causes that?' asked her man. But after careful observation of the birds and the bees they figured out that when two people lovingly join as one, then that is the moment when they are at their most creative—creative like God is creative and one like God is one.

The first command God gave to the human race as recorded in the Bible was 'Be fruitful and multiply', which means have sex and lots of babies. That wasn't a difficult command to obey, so they went at it like rabbits, and we haven't stopped obeying God's command ever since! And that's where babies come from. That was how the reflection of God's image was multiplied. Love—together—one. And that's how we all happened, every last one of us, part of a trinity, just like God. Families—the basic building blocks of society, united by love.

Creative

Which brings me to the obvious conclusion that God is *creative*.

I am creative. I can make stuff. Give me a few blocks of wood and I can build a house. But the Bible doesn't dub God merely a builder or designer, but a *creator*. That suggests starting from scratch, from nothing but a blank sheet of paper—and not even paper. 'Through him all things were made; without him nothing was made that has been made.' I sure warm to the thought that everything is not just a chance, one big cosmic accident, the lucky result of an infinite roll of the dice. Perhaps, then, my life does have purpose.

I have to admit that on first reading I did get a bit sceptical over the early pages of the Bible. That part about everything being created in less than a week? Bit of a rush job, eh? But come to think of it, whoever wrote the early pages of the Bible would have considered his readership. If he'd come up with the general theory of relativity and cosmological models of a consistently expanding universe, the eyes of some of his early readers might have glazed over. So perhaps simplicity was just the ticket. 'God said: Let there be…'

But I can't help but wonder exactly *how* it all happened. *How* was the world made? Scientists are still working on the answer, and I look forward to reading their final conclusions. But I am wondering if perhaps *how* is not as important as *who*. *Who* made the world? The Bible may be a little fuzzy about the *how*, but it's very clear on the *who*: 'In the beginning God created the heavens and the earth.'

When something technical in my home goes pear-shaped I am generally more interested in who made it than in *how* it was made. Just tell me *who* to blame and *who* can I call to fix it. Never mind the details of how and when it was manufactured. Perhaps the same principle applies to my dysfunctional self. I don't much care *how* I was made, just tell me *who* will fix me.

But I confess I am still intrigued by the *how* question. *How* did God make me?

The Bible just says he used words. He spoke it. If the pen is mightier than the sword, then perhaps words are mightier than a Big Bang, certainly more precise.

I count almost a dozen times in the first chapter of the Bible that God spoke, promised, commanded, verbalised things and voila! Here we all are: *Let there be day and night. Let there be earth and sky. Let there be dry land and ocean. Let there be vegetation and animals.*

Love

I could imagine that God is nice, even kind. But as usual the Bible has me beat. *God is love.* That's what the Bible says. Simple as that. If love makes the world go round and if Tolstoy had it right when he wrote that 'love is the only reality in the world', and if love is the stuff of which I am made, and if love is patient and kind and never fails, and if God is love, and if I am designed to be like God, then I'm in. God is just what I'd choose to be like. That is the one thing I am after.

Pale Reflection

No wonder I feel a bit of a let-down when I look in the mirror. I am nothing like God. But I'm a God-wannabe. I don't mean I want his job, just that I admire what he's like.

If God is infinite, I am pint-sized. But I'm growing.

If God is eternal, I am a flash in the pan. Yet I have to admit that I do hanker for something more. An afterlife perhaps?

If God is smart, I am ignorant. But I'm curious.

If God is always everywhere, I'm stuck in the here and now. But I hanker to know what may be round the next corner.

If God is strong, I am puny. But I love to operate big, oily machinery to shift tons of dirt.

If God is good, I am at best mediocre. Yet my conscience goads me to improve.

If God is love… Well, yes. To love and be loved is my ambition. But do I bear any resemblance to that definition of love—'patient and kind, humble and gracious, unselfish and even-tempered'? Am I 'quick to forgive and forget'? Do I 'always protect, always trust, always hope, always persevere'? Does my 'love never fail'? Well, that's a joke. But I sure would like that to describe me. That's the man I want to be, and if that's what God is like, then I want to be like him.

If God is creative, I can paint. I do walls and ceilings, but I'm no Michelangelo. But then again, I'm not a complete failure when it comes to creativity. With the help of my wife, I have created some gorgeous babies: three of them, little beauties, works of art, though I say so myself! That's creative, isn't it?

If society needs a reboot, if we are looking for that one thing to alter our trajectory, we could do worse than getting the focus back on the basics, right? One building block at a time. One family at a time. Mine for starters.

So how is my family to be restored? Perhaps it has something to do with getting back to our original purpose: reflecting the image of God, the original archetype we were designed to replicate.

Do I want my family to reflect God's loving, together, one-yet-three-ness? You bet your sweet life I do. I want all the broken pieces of my family to be reformed as one loving whole. *That one thing.*

Distortion

But if God is love and we are his mirror, where did hate and disappointment come from?

Perhaps we're reflecting something other than God—the larger-than-life heroes we idolise in the movies;

normal behaviour as seen on TV; the stuff that fills the garage, things we worship.

Maybe we don't reflect anything other than ourselves, what we see in the mirror. A reflection of a reflection of a reflection that gradually fades into obscurity.

It's conceivable that the image of God we are seeking to reflect is actually a parody of God. Perhaps we have fallen for the notion that God is violent and vengeful, that he would be pleased if we imposed our religious views on others, inflicting on them violence or even death should they refuse to convert. Religion. Frankly, if God were like that, I would choose to be an atheist and proud of it!

But I don't see God that way at all. I look out of my window and see snow-capped mountains and deep green valleys, birds and flowers, 'and I think to myself, what a wonderful world'. The Bible concludes the chapter on creation by saying 'God saw all that he had made, and it was very good.' And I for one can't help but agree with him. So, the God who made such a wonderful world can't be half bad himself, can he?

So why then is the human race such a distortion of God's image? Why does shit happen? Why the misery and pain? Why do people abuse each other, rape, steal, murder, wage war? God isn't like that, so how come we are? If we are supposed to be reflections, jerked like puppets this way and that by the object we can only replicate, then someone must have cut the strings! Who cut them?

No Strings Attached

What if God himself cut the strings? Perhaps an essential part of reflecting God is being free to choose. What chance is there for human dignity if we can't say 'No'? To love is a choice, a good choice that I can be proud of, grateful for, but if I had no option but to love, would my wife feel special? If love is to be a free choice, it must have an alternative—indifference at the very least, but hate as an extreme. Good would cease to be good were it not equally possible to be mediocre or even flat-out bad. And 'Yes' would have no value were I incapable of saying 'no'.

If you love something, you set it free, right? So perhaps the very fact that I am not perfect suggests that God must love me. He has set me free to choose. I have dignity! To love my neighbour is my choice. I don't have to love him. I could be indifferent towards him. I might even hate him. But I am free to make that decision. So, part of my reflecting God's image is that I am free to reflect him *or not*, as I choose.

The Knowledge

Early on, the Bible tells a story that illustrates the origin of free choice. Humans were living in a paradise, a park where everything was perfect. There were no signs saying 'Do not walk on the grass', 'No trespassing' and 'No alcohol'. Everything was OK, permitted, even encouraged. God said, 'You are free to eat from any tree in the garden.'

There was only one thing that was off limits—just one. It was a tree in the middle of the park tagged 'The tree of the knowledge of good and evil'. While God told people, 'You are free to eat from any tree in the garden', he put that one tree out of bounds: 'but you must not eat from the tree of the knowledge of good and evil, for when you eat from it you will surely die.'

Had I been in that garden, I think I would have been fascinated by that tree. I imagine myself sitting on a park bench, gazing at it. Just the fact that it was forbidden would have whet my appetite. The tantalising thought that there was a *knowledge*, a secret that I didn't know, an experience that I hadn't had, would have driven me crazy. 'Got to have the *knowledge!*'

And anyway, what could the warning be about? What would 'surely die' feel like? Up until that point, according to the Bible, no one had ever done that and lived to tell the tale.

Then along comes this snake in the grass who whispers, 'Did God really say "You must not eat from any tree in the garden"?'

Well, no, actually. He had said it was OK to eat from any tree in the garden, all except this one tree, that is.

That would result in something called 'surely die'.

'Nonsense!' insisted the snake. 'God knows that when you eat it your eyes will be opened, and you will be like God, knowing good and evil.' Ah. The knowledge! It would make you like God! Yes, indeed, there would be something divine, sophisticated, liberating about being able to make my own decisions about what is good and what is evil. But that would only come at the expense of my saying one little 'No!' to God. Until then creation had only ever said 'Yes' to God, and it owed its very existence to that positive response. To refuse the word of the creator would surely reverse the process of creation, the essence of antimatter. Spell 'LIVE' backwards and you get 'EVIL'. Could that explain why 'surely die' and 'evil' are linked?

I wonder what I would have done faced with that original choice? I fear I would have risked it and made the same mistake as those original humans.

Ignorance is Bliss…

…or so they say, and they might well be right since the story goes on to tell how all kinds of trouble came with the *knowledge*. Evil! They had long known what *good* was. Everything they had ever experienced up until that day had only ever been good, *very good*. But now? *Evil*?

Close on its heels came *guilt*. Suddenly the happy

couple felt embarrassed just for being in the buff. They had never worn clothes and never given it a second thought, except perhaps on chilly winter evenings. Shame made them hide in the bushes when God next came knocking. With the *knowledge* came a whole entourage of unpleasantness—dishonour, disgrace, scandal, regret, humiliation, self-loathing, indignity, sorrow, grief—things that I'll bet they wished they didn't know. But the *knowledge* was a package deal, a bundle: take one, take all. And the sad story is that it sapped the life out of them and has been doing the same to us all ever since.

In Greek mythology, Pandora is alleged to have been confronted with a choice of good or evil. For her, it wasn't a tree but a box, given by the gods with the instruction that it was not to be opened in any circumstances. But in their malicious generosity, those naughty gods also gave her the gift of curiosity. She had to *know* what was in the wretched box! The *knowledge*. So, inevitably, she opened it and evil escaped and filled the whole world.

So, whether I blame Eve or Pandora, the end result is the same. Evil has slimed me and my family. Hate has reared its ugly head and spat in the eye of love.

Evil

Is *evil* just the absence of good, I ask myself. The absence of love is indifference, but hate is somehow more than that. And the absence of good suggests some kind of moral vacuum, but evil is more than that. It is cruel, vile and destructive. Evil is rape and child abuse. Evil is torture, murder, war. I visited Rwanda soon after the genocide and saw the bones of those who had been violently hacked to death by their neighbours, still lying where they fell. Don't tell me that evil is merely the absence of good! If knowing evil is the *knowledge*, I'd sooner be ignorant.

But being accused of being ignorant is the goad that forces me to seek the knowledge. 'Don't be naïve! Go ahead and live a little! How do you know that evil is really so bad unless you try it?' I've heard it all before and been shamed into giving it a go. The first humans fell for that line, so why wouldn't I?

Anyway, there's something attractive about evil. 'Keep out!' is an irresistible invitation. 'Don't walk on the grass!' is a come on.

What's more, once you've done it, evil seems to be addictive. I can understand what substance abuse can do to a family, for it has done it to mine. But there the addiction is a chemical dependence that must be satisfied. But where's the chemistry in child abuse, wife beating, pornography, gambling? These are all behaviours that have nothing to do with chemicals, but are just as addictive and equally destructive to loving families. Yes, evil is a cruel tyrant that demands its pound of flesh. It is comparatively easy to say no to the first bite, but the more I eat the more difficult it is to resist.

And while we are on the subject, evil grows. One rotten apple can spoil the whole barrel, as Granny used to say. It took only one little bullet, propelled from one little gun, activated by one little trigger, pulled by one little finger, belonging to one little man, to start World War I, but the evil grew until 17 million were dead. What a selfish little bozo Gavrilo Princip must have been to assassinate Archduke Franz Ferdinand that fateful June day in 1914, but I bet he had no idea what he was unleashing when his evil little finger pulled that innocent little trigger. Yes, evil grows.

Evil is devious. 'Did God really say, "You must not eat from any tree in the garden"?' Well, no. He didn't say any such thing. But those two original humans were tricked by the confusion of the words. If they said 'Yes', then God was down on eating, or any kind of fun. If they replied 'No', then go right ahead and eat your fill!

Evil mutates. What may have started with apples soon became oranges and bananas, a whole orchard of trouble. To ban the one tree required one simple no-no—relatively easy to identify and avoid. But what happens when the mutation goes ape and there are numerous dangerous trees offering all kinds of attractive but poisonous fruits? Life becomes a minefield of pain. Because I love my children, I warned them to keep their little poky fingers out of the power outlets, their wet little tongues off the frozen railings, to stay off the ice on the pond in the park, not to play hockey in traffic. But there are a dozen other things I didn't think to warn them about: giant hogweed, poison ivy, plastic bags over the head, to name but three. Evil has many varieties, and they all kill. 'When you eat of it you will surely die.'

'What's wrong with just looking? Everybody does it. You only live once!' I suppose all that is true. Nothing is wrong with *just* looking, but does it ever stop there? And, yes. You do only live once; but in the end everybody dies… Thanks, Evil.

Prohibitions

Once evil had mutated, the one command not to eat that one forbidden fruit no longer covered all the life-threatening dangers. But how was anyone to recognise evil as evil? Trial and error? A kind of moral roulette? Painful. So the Bible says that God spelled it out with words, written down this time, engraved on slabs of rock so there could be no crossings out or alterations.

A man named Moses is introduced in the second section of the Bible. He arrives, staggering down a mountain, looking a lot like Charlton Heston, with a slab of hieroglyphics under each arm. He put them in a box for safe keeping, like something out of Indiana Jones.

These hieroglyphics spelled out ten commands, Ten Words, ten *Let there not be's*. They had the same punch as his original *Let there be's*, but now instead of being phrased positively—*Let there be*—they were negatives—*Let there NOT be*. In contrast to the positive words of creation that gave life, the Ten Words gave ten prohibitions against that which would destroy life.

Where once there had been only one *Let there not be* warning sign on that one poisonous tree, now there were ten warning signs, hung on ten poisonous trees—and eating fruit from any one of them would start you down the path to *surely die*.

Ten Words

1. Don't love anything more than God. 2. Don't worship man-made stuff. 3. Don't abuse God's good name. 4. Don't work without taking a day off every week. 5. Don't dishonour your parents. 6. Don't kill. 7. Don't cheat on your spouse. 8. Don't steal. 9. Don't lie. 10. Don't crave what you haven't got.

Now, I get the obvious dangers from which many of those prohibitions might save a guy—*don't kill, don't steal*—but some, in contrast, seem trivial. *Don't work without taking a day off every week*, for example. What's so important about a day off? But then I check the stats. Way more people die every year from stress-related illness (heart attack, stroke, etc.) than from getting murdered. What's more, not taking a day off costs more than it gains; 75% of the cost of health care in Western countries can be attributed to stress. So pardon me for questioning it. If I were smart enough to take a real day out from the rat race every week, I might just live a longer and happier life and enable others around me to do likewise.

Don't crave what you haven't got is another prohibition that appears inconsequential. What's wrong with window-shopping? Discontent, I suppose; imagining that my neighbour's grass is greener than mine; always wanting something else; never being satisfied; addicted to more, more, more! OK. Point taken. So, being discontented is not a healthy way to live.

The three words at the top of the list seem to have something to do with religion: *Don't love anything more than God. Don't worship man-made stuff. Don't abuse God's good name.*

Don't worship man-made stuff is probably a warning against materialism, but more likely it is talking about obsession with symbols and icons, maybe even the buildings and institutions of which religious folks seem to be so proud. *Not abusing God's good name* is probably forbidding the use of the odd curse word—rude, but nothing to get hung about. But on second thoughts, what about the names and denominations our forefathers invented to brand their favourite man-made religious traditions? That hasn't done much to give God a good name, has it? In fact, it damages his reputation for being *one*. And worse, the adherents of these denominations fight like cats, even seem ready to kill or be killed to defend their own chosen brand. Now, that kind of thing has done some serious damage to our peaceful little human coexistence. It has been one of the prime causes of conflict and war in the history of mankind. No wonder this comes high on the list of no-nos.

In Rwanda, religion played a big part in the genocide. 'Which God do you worship?' we were asked by a gang of young men on a busy street in Kigali. We were there to help in the reconciliation process, so we insisted that there is only one God. But they assured us that this was not the case in Rwanda. 'We have an Anglican god, a Pentecostal god, a Baptist god, a Catholic god. Here we have many gods.' Perhaps that explained the confusion that cost the lives of so many who took refuge in such churches from the horrors that followed.

As Gandhi is quoted to have commented: 'If it were not for the Christians, I would be one.' No wonder the Ten Words include near the top of the list a warning against the man-made institutions, religions and denominations that give the one God the reputation of having a split personality.

Is God himself religious? Is he a Catholic? Is he a Protestant? Is he Orthodox? Is he Christian? Is he Muslim? We may choose to be branded by one or other of those names, but does God? And if God declines to brand himself with any of those labels, and if I am supposed to be like him, then why would I not follow his good example? If we would only observe the first three words of the big Ten, that alone might minimise the likelihood of World War III. But actually observing all ten would make the world a safer, happier place.

Just Imagine…

… Peace and contentment instead of always craving more; everyone trusting each other, with our word being our bond, instead of lies and suspicion. How about business being about giving—giving good service and generous dealing—rather than screwing the other guy? And imagine if the family were a safe place where we were loved and felt secure right through our old age and the kids were certain that Mum and Dad would always be home—together. How about forgiveness and self-sacrifice in place of killing and violence; respect for parents and all in authority instead of anarchy and hooliganism; peaceful, balanced lives with a healthy rhythm of work and rest with time to sniff the roses, rather than the rat race with a heart attack at the finish? And what if God's name were honoured rather than being used as a curse word or sliced and diced by religion; the Creator who made everything being thanked rather than obsession with man-made stuff; God being loved rather than the subject of endless arguments and the source of wars over religion.

A world like that, as prescribed by the Ten Words, sounds good to me.

I see further on in the Bible that the Ten Words are summed up in one sentence: 'Love God and love your neighbour as you love yourself.' Wasn't that why God made us in the first place—to love? And wasn't that how we all arrived on this planet? Isn't that the one thing we are seeking?

Is there an alternative? Well, yes: indifference or, ultimately, hate. But where would that lead? 'When you eat of it you will surely die' was the warning on that tree that offered us the *knowledge*. Bit harsh, though, don't you think? Some kind of scale of values with punishments that fit the crime might be better, *n'est-ce pas*?

Crime and Punishment

But the Bible describes God's consequences not just as a fine or a term behind bars. They are absolute: 'surely die'. Perhaps the absolute nature of the consequences suggests the absolute nature of the crimes. If it is absolutely never ever loving to kill, lie, steal, cheat, etc., then we must absolutely never ever do any of that nasty stuff and the only way to guarantee that we absolutely won't is for us to *surely die*, leaving us with absolutely no possibility whatsoever of persisting down that path or taking others with us. Can't get more absolute than that, right? Evil is evil. Hate is hate. No is no. Death is death. End of.

But I suppose death isn't always such a powerful deterrent against evil. It might even offer a quick escape from the pain of the here and now. Come to think of it, some people have been induced to perpetrate all kinds of evil with the promise of a glorious death, especially with seventy-two virgins on the other side to sweeten the deal. So, just in case death isn't enough of a deterrent, the Bible hints at a second death: 'After the killing of the body, he has power to throw you into hell where the worms never die and the fire never goes out.'

But I have to confess that I'm not a great fan of rules and consequences. Perhaps that's a hangover from my school days, when my life was controlled by rules, and the consequences for non-compliance were usually painful. They ranged from a rap on my knuckles to a thrashing on my backside.

I received such chastisements on several painful occasions during those days, usually for minor offences such as smoking. I guess the deterrent was effective, since I don't smoke to this day. I tried bribing my kids not to smoke with the promise of a car if they were still clean when they reached twenty-one. Didn't work. Perhaps a thrashing would have been more effective.

I remember a young lad, a friend of my son Dan, coming to stay with us for a few weeks. His dad had abandoned the family, and his mother, now a single mum, found it impossible to control her dear little ten-year-old. So we gave her a break. Little Olly ran amok in our house from the terrible moment he arrived. Early on, I laid down the law, spelling out a few simple house rules. He used them as a list of suggestions of fun things to do. I did my best to be nice. Didn't work. So then I warned him that while he was in our house I would treat him like one of my own children. He would get the wooden spoon to his backside if he refused to obey. The threat didn't work. He continued his rampage, making everyone's life a misery. Then I caught him and Dan in the act. And I whacked them both where the sun never shines. I guess I would be arrested for doing that today, but those were different times! Olly was silent and surly for the next day or two, but then the sun came out. He became friendly and fun to have in our home.

The night before he was due to go home, I was

putting him and Dan to bed. 'Good night, Dad', says Dan.

'Can I call you Dad?' asks Olly. 'You see, I really like it here.'

'How so?' I ask, feeling rotten for having whacked him.

'I feel safe here. I think it is because you stop me from doing wrong things.'

I guess God is like that. If he is, then perhaps I am safe here too. God loves me enough to stop me doing wrong things, things that are never, ever loving. Perhaps that is one of the ways God has of saying to me, 'I love you.'

Saying it with Flowers

I can't imagine why God would love me. In fact, I can't imagine why he would even notice I exist. But he seems to have put a lot of thought into creating me, so I guess he does at least know I am here. He's put me in a wonderful world and given me the equipment to enjoy it all: eyes to see colours, ears to hear music and laughter, taste buds to make eating and drinking enjoyable, a nose to sniff the roses and nerve endings for good feelings. All that suggests that he must at least like me. And he's warned me to avoid things that might hurt me, so he must care. But love? Love demands more than giving nice things, more than establishing rules for my safety, more than words.

My wife loves me. She tells me so almost every day. She brings me coffee in bed on a Sunday morning. And I love her too.

I love Henry, my dog. I give him food twice a day and a treat at bedtime. I pat him and rub his tummy when he rolls on his back. I give him rules, boundaries to stop him running into the road and getting squashed by a truck. But does he really know I love him?

Ants are tricky. How would an ant know I loved it? They are hard to pet and their tummies are too small to rub. And what do ants like for treats? Yes, I provide them with a home under the pile of pine needles in the back yard and I do my best not to disturb them. But do they know I love them? The truth is that I don't—especially when they come into my kitchen and armies of the little beggars carry off my sugar. But supposing I was dumb enough to want to tell them that I loved them. How would I do it? I see no alternative but that I'd have to join them, become one of them, move into the anthill, learn to speak ant, rub feelers with them, give them a hug. I could give them little granules of sugar, forbid them to march over the driveway lest my wife should run them over, warn them about those little round tins of pesticide. I'd show them!

So, what about God? How could he tell me he loves me?

Christmas

I love to receive gifts, especially the really thoughtful ones that show how much the giver loves me. I'm not wild about socks or ties; stuff from the hardware store is more like it. And I love to see the faces of my grandkids when they open their presents at Christmas.

Much of what I read in the Bible I can't remember, but there is one sentence about love and giving that sticks. It runs something like this: 'God loves the world so much that he gave his only son.' Every year at Christmas we follow God's good example by giving gifts as a way of saying 'I love you'. That insignificant gift of a baby delivered in a barn in an insignificant village somewhere in Israel is the inspiration for all that explosion of seasonal generosity.

God could have said 'I love you' in a thousand ways, but it looks like he chose to say it personally. Words, yes, but words gift-wrapped in human skin.

I found several accounts of Christmas in the Bible, most of them including shepherds and wise men. One of the accounts seemed a little more abstruse, but it caught my interest because it picks up on the recurring theme of *words*.

The Bible started out with words credited with being God's means of creation: 'Let there be'. Then, when people began doing bad stuff, God gave Ten Words to stop them hurting each other: 'Let there not be'. And now, here in the Christmas story, words are given a human skin: 'The Word made human'. The story is expressed as though it were words being birthed as human. 'Anthropomorphism' is how the wordsmiths would express the process, but the Bible simply says: 'The Word became human and lived among us.' The Word born as a baby in a barn in Bethlehem. Who or what is *the Word*? I don't get the impression that this is just referring to sounds from a mouth or scribbles from a pen. For a start, *Word* has a capital 'W'. *'The Word was with God and the Word was God.'*

So here's the progression. Words create good things: 'Let there be'. Words forbid bad things: 'Let there not be'. Now the Word becomes human: *Jesus*. And as I read on, I get a picture of what kind of a person Jesus turned out to be when he grew up. The definition of love that I first started with sounds a lot like him.

> *Love is patient, love is kind. It does not envy, it does not boast, it is not proud. It is not rude, it is not self-seeking, it is not easily angered, it keeps no record of wrongs. Love does not delight in evil but rejoices with the truth. It always protects, always trusts, always hopes, always perseveres. Love never fails.*

Yes, Jesus seems to tick all the boxes. So, in a word, Jesus is love personified. The Ten Words say what love is not. One Word says what love is. I have the outer limits of love described in Ten Words defining the no-go area beyond which things are never ever loving, and I have the same shape fleshed out in Jesus, 'the Word become human'—a magnificent portrait of love in a human skin.

Five Senses

Words, when all I can do is hear them, quickly fly out of my forgetful little brain. But if I can see them *written* as well as hear them *spoken*, I am much more likely get their message. But supposing my other senses kicked in as well, and I could feel them like a hug, taste them like a tankard of ale, smell them like a bouquet of flowers? Well then, how could I fail to get the message? Perfect communication.

So what if this is God's way of becoming an ant, conveying his message of 'I love you' to human little me in words that I can recognise with each of my five senses? Now that would be Words with a capital 'W'.

I have always loved the story of Christmas. Magic! But the story continues, and the baby grows up.

There are four biographies of Jesus in the New Testament part of the Bible, all slightly different but all telling roughly the same story. He grows up to be a normal blue-collar kind of guy, a carpenter. But when he turns thirty the fun begins. Communication becomes 20/20, in brilliant colour.

Taste

The first time it happened was at a party, a wedding reception to be precise. Jesus and his buddies were all guests, and they had such a good time that the drink ran out; all the champers gone. Well, that wouldn't do.

Water came out of wells back then, not taps, so to facilitate hygiene, the caterers had laid on half a dozen tubs of water. By the time all the guests had rinsed off, the water may have been getting a little scummy. 'Take some of that water to the best man so he can have a taste,' says Jesus, pointing at the tubs.

Some wretched server was stuck with the unenviable task of pouring that grubby water into the best man's glass. He must have expected a rollicking, but instead, 'Excellent bouquet!' and everyone agreed that this was simply the best wine ever. So they all drank to the happy couple, to the bride and groom, the man and the woman whose loving union could now reproduce a third, a family, a trinity, the image of God! I'll drink to that.

'I love you!' said God, and they all tasted it.

Feel

Leprosy is a rotten disease. It kills off all the nerve endings so the person who's infected can't feel anything. A rat could chew your finger off in the night and you'd know nothing about it until you tried to scratch your nose in the morning. Or if you inadvertently sat too close to the fire, the first you would know about it would be the smell of cooking. But the worst problem of all is that leprosy is highly contagious. Back in Bible days, if you were diagnosed with the dreaded plague, you were banished from your family—and indeed, from all human company. You were treated as an untouchable.

There must have been many lepers in Jesus' day. He encountered one of them on the outskirts of town. 'Help me!' he yelled from a hygienic distance when he saw Jesus. To the horror of all the onlookers, Jesus walked right up to him, reached out and shook his hand—gave him a hug. First time he'd been touched in years. Flesh restored like a newborn's.

'I love you!' said God, and he felt it.

Hear

To be shut up in a silent world must be a lonely prison. No music, no laughter, no conversation. If you can't even hear your own voice, you have no idea if the sounds you are making are intelligible.

There was a guy like that, just over the lake from where Jesus lived. A crowd of people were milling round when Jesus met him. So, sensitive to the man's self-consciousness, Jesus beckoned for him to follow to a quiet corner. Standard comments about the weather and 'How's your father?' would not have helped, so Jesus just poked his fingers into the man's deaf ears, then spat on his palm and touched the useless tongue. 'Be opened' Jesus whispered.

'Oh, thank you!' came the clearly audible reply. 'Thank you very much.'

'I love you!' said God, and he heard it.

See

I often wonder if it would be worse to be blind or to be deaf: darkness or silence? I am happy with neither, thank you very much. But supposing I had been born blind, how would I understand the word 'light', or 'blue', 'red' or 'sunrise'? No comprehension at all. So how could I see that God loves me?

It was a young guy like that, sitting begging on the street, who caught Jesus' attention.

'Why is this lad blind?' someone asks. 'Was it his fault, or his parents?' Got to blame somebody, right?

'Nobody's fault,' Jesus replies. 'But watch this…' So saying, he spits in the dust, mixes it into mud and then rubs it into the blind guy's eyes. Well, yuck! 'Go wash your face,' Jesus tells him. My guess? He was off like a blue streak to find a washroom. A pool had to suffice, but suddenly he saw blue sky reflected in the shimmering water and a brown face reflected back at him. *His face*. A reflection of the image of God clearly visible for the first time.

'I love you!' said God, and he saw it—20/20.

Smell

I love the smell of freshly mown grass, of lilacs, of cedar logs. But when you are dead, you can't do much smelling. It's other people who do the smelling, and you are the smell. Jesus went to a funeral, but arrived late. The guy had been dead and buried for four days, since in that hot climate you start to rot pronto. They hadn't actually buried the guy, though, just put him on a slab in a tomb with a rock over the entrance.

'Shift that rock!' says Jesus unexpectedly—an unusual demand in a cemetery.

'But he'll stink by now', someone argued. They did what he said.

'Come out here!' shouts Jesus into the black hole. And out he came, smiling and breathing like a spring breeze.

'I love you!' said God, and they all smelt its fragrance.

Perfect Communication

Yes, all five senses saying 'I love you'.

Great stories! I could be into doing those kind of good deeds, helping hurting people—if only I had the ability. I get a glow when I just drop a coin in a panhandler's hat! So I'm thinking that for Jesus, it must have been quite the rush, hiking around the planet like superman, championing the downtrodden and disadvantaged, healing the sick, raising the dead and such. What's more, all that was guaranteed to boost his approval rating. He could have run for president. Everyone loved him! Who wouldn't?

But actually, not everyone did love him, and it's not so easy loving people who don't appreciate you. I'm happy to help a guy out, but what if he tells me to get lost? And what am I supposed to do with the arrogant, the rude, the surly so-and-so's who hang around street corners, the guy who cuts into my line of traffic, the dictators, the wife beaters, the child abusers, the racists, the bigots? Am I supposed to love them too?

Apparently, Jesus had some choice things to say on that subject:

> *If someone punches you in the face, turn the other cheek. If someone sues the pants off you, give him the shirt off your back. If someone bad-mouths you, compliment him! If someone takes advantage of your generosity, write it off; think of it as a gift. If he wrongs you, forgive him. If he persists in wronging you, persist in forgiving him until*

> *he gives up. And if he never gives up? Always let forgiveness have the last word. Love knows no limit. It will outdo hatred every time.*

Or at least, that was the gist of it.

The bottom line was the most outrageous demand ever: 'Love your enemies.' But if you loved your enemies, they wouldn't be your enemies, would they? Perhaps that's his point.

Here's what I am wondering: Would Jesus be able to continue being so nice if he found himself dropping in the popularity polls, if people stopped appreciating the kind things he was doing for them? Well, the story continues…

Decline

Drop in popularity he did. Big time.

It was from the religious folk that trouble originated. Seems they were upset when Jesus made out he was God. It wasn't that he came right out and said 'I am God', but it was the hints he dropped that got up their noses. He was forever referring to himself as 'I am', a label everyone knew to be reserved exclusively for God. And he called God 'my Father'. What a nerve!

Another irritating habit he had was failing to put down bad people. Religious leaders are supposed to condemn sinners, right? But Jesus would pronounce them 'forgiven', and only God had the clout to do that. And surely God had made it clear from the beginning that if you do evil you would 'surely die'. So, if God had set the rules, who was this upstart to mess with the status quo and start letting people off the hook? Was he suggesting that 'surely die' was cancelled? 'I don't think so,' was their conclusion. And furthermore, perhaps it was Jesus who should be the one to do the surely dying. So they arrested him and brought him in for questioning.

Key Question

The big kahuna, the high priest, made it clear from the get-go that they weren't upset about the good stuff he had been doing, the healings and such, but they were offended by his implying that he was God. But they couldn't really believe that even Jesus would be so arrogant as to make such a claim, so they put him in the dock and made him swear to tell the truth, the whole truth and nothing but the truth. Then they pinned him with the all-important question: 'Are you the Son of God?'

'Yes, I am,' he replied.

Well, you can't get plainer than that.

Of course, smart lawyers can always twist the truth and tie you in knots with their confusing questions: 'Is it not true that the Bible teaches that we are all sons of God? And are not the angels sometimes referred to as "sons of God"?' But evidently no such lawyers confused anybody. What they all heard was a straight-up claim that he was the Son of God—royal family; heir apparent to God Almighty. And that was not the answer they were wanting to hear. They did a lot of yelling and spitting and name-calling. Then they all agreed that he would have to die—'surely die'. But it would have to be legal and above board, sanctioned by the proper authorities.

Supreme Court

So, they dragged him off to see the governor and demanded he be executed. Pontius Pilate didn't care much for the niceties of religion and was more concerned with the political fallout. The accused might pose a threat to his boss, the Emperor in Rome, so Pilate cross-examined him. But Jesus didn't argue the point or plead innocence. He just stayed mum. That is, until Pilate barked at him in frustration: 'Don't you realise who I am? I have the power of life and death. I can have you executed or let you walk.'

'Actually,' Jesus replied, 'you wouldn't have any power over me at all unless it had been given you from above…'

Who was this guy talking about, Pilate must have wondered. Who had given him, Pilate, Governor of Judea, power from above? The only one above him in the chain of command was the Emperor. The only one, that is, if you discounted God. But should God be discounted? One of the few doctrines of the local religion that Pilate must have appreciated was submission to authority: 'all authority is established by God', they believed. So arguing that God had appointed him would have been handy when trying to keep order in a disorderly but God-fearing society.

But the prisoner wasn't done talking: 'And so it is the one who handed me over to you who carries the final responsibility for this sin.' Now who was he on about? It had been the High Priest who had just handed Jesus over to be killed. But was Jesus merely blaming the High Priest, or was he suggesting that this was somehow God's idea, that God had ordained that this man be handed over for sentencing in Pilate's court?

Perhaps that was it. He was holding God ultimately responsible, putting God in the frame. I imagine Pilate had heard many excuses from all kinds of desperate criminals, but pinning this on God himself must have taken the biscuit.

But I suppose when all is said and done, someone has to be blamed, someone held responsible for pain and injustice. And sometimes it's hard to tell if God or man should carry the can. Many a time I have been bent out of shape over injustice, angry with people who do wrong—but furious with God for not stopping them. The Holocaust, for example—those dirty Nazis! But where was God that he didn't stop them? So I can't blame Jesus for lashing out. I mean, if God is almighty, why didn't he rescue Jesus from what they were about to do to him, especially since I read that Jesus had begged God for deliverance just the previous evening? Many a desperate mother has prayed her knees black and blue, begging God to spare her sick child, only to be broken-hearted when the kid dies. If God is so loving, how come he so often seems to stand idly by doing nothing in the face of rape, violence, murder, genocide and the like?

Perhaps he's not so loving after all. Perhaps he's not as almighty as I thought, and he's just not able to do anything to help. Perhaps he's not so smart as I imagined, and he doesn't know how much we are hurting down here. Or perhaps he just doesn't care. In which case, should I be looking for another God?

Final Responsibility

But then again, there's another way of looking at all this. What if there are no strings attached to God's gift of free choice? No matter how badly we abuse it, he won't take it back? A gift's a gift. End of.

And what if Jesus wasn't simply lashing out in frustration, but was actually laying the responsibility at God's door: 'the final responsibility for this sin'? After all, it was God who made Pilate and the Emperor in Rome and those slimy priests, and it was God who established them in the position to judge Jesus, since 'there is no authority except that which God has established'. So, was Jesus laying on God 'the final responsibility for this sin', and perhaps all the other sins with it, mine included?

Was God insulted that Jesus fingered him?

Was Jesus bothered that he was the one left to carry the can on God's behalf?

What kind of justice was that? Who was he, Jesus from Nazareth, anyway, that he had to be the one to get nailed? An innocent third party? An exemplary human being selected to be some kind of scapegoat? An angel sent to Earth to be God's stooge? And if so, what kind of a monster must God be to lay this responsibility—his own responsibility—on an innocent bystander, let alone on his own kith and kin—on his son?

Ultimate Justice

Only one thing seems to make any sense of all this, only one explanation that doesn't paint God as a monster. Jesus was exactly who he claimed to be: the 'I am'; the Son of God; the second member of the trinity; the one with the authority to forgive sins. In which case, Jesus was not an innocent third party but God himself, shouldering the responsibility for having made us free to choose good or evil. And what followed was God's way of accepting the consequences—'surely die'.

If so, that sounds to me like ultimate justice and ultimate love, from start to finish. God loves me and sets me free to make my own choices. But God loves me, so he spells out right from wrong, warning me of the consequences of choosing wrong. When I inevitably make the wrong choices, God recognises that someone has to surely die. Should it be me for choosing evil, or should it be God for making it possible for me to choose evil? God or me? God so loves me that he chooses to be the one to take the rap so I can live free.

But how can God actually do the dying, seeing as God is immortal and lives forever? The answer is that the Father sent the Son, his alter ego, to become a mortal man so he could take the fall for sin—'surely die'.

The trinity: Father, Son and Spirit in cahoots. The Father gives the order. The Son obeys. The Spirit affirms. The three in agreement. Done deal!

But I can't help but feel guilty. I mean, I've made some dumb choices, hurt a lot of people. My conscience stings. So, can I just shrug it off now and say it's God's responsibility? Tell that nagging little voice inside me that it's OK, not to worry, I'm not to blame? Well, I don't think so, thank you very much. I am to blame—and I know it. And that's a weight I find it hard to bear, one that sometimes drives me to the bottle and will doubtless one day drive me to the grave. But that's exactly where this story leads: to the grave.

The story continues, frequently portrayed by artists of paint and film, and represented by trinkets of all kinds. Frankly, the movies turn my stomach. And the trinkets are ghoulish, to say the least. Imagine a loved one, executed on the electric chair, forever commemorated by a gold electric chair bauble hung on a chain around your neck. Macabre! But that's gold crosses for you. Or how about hot electric chair buns at Easter?

Execution

It took some legal wrangling and political manoeuvring, but in the end those religious bigots got their way, and a squad of soldiers were dispatched to do the deed.

They didn't hang criminals in those days, and anything as humane as the electric chair was thousands of years from being invented. So they gave him the standard treatment. They nailed his arms to a two-by-six and hung him up on a pole.

Television not yet having been invented, such executions were a popular spectator sport, so crowds of people turned out to watch the whole grisly show. They all knew who the condemned man was and exactly why their religious fathers were hanging him out to dry, so some bright spark came up with the obvious question: 'Hey, Jesus!' he yelled up at him. 'If you are the Son of God, how come you don't just float down off that cross?' If he could walk on water and raise the dead, would it have been so hard to extricate himself from a couple of six-inch spikes?

'Nobody is taking my life from me,' Jesus gasped. 'I am doing this of my own free choice, giving up my life so that many others won't have to die.'

Then another person started in on him. This guy directed his jibes over Jesus' head, at God himself: 'God, this man claims that you are his father. So if you love him at all, right now might be a good time to show it!' Well, that brought a howl of laughter from the crowd, but no reply from above, no thunderbolt, no big foot coming down from the sky.

Why not?

Here's how the Bible explains it:

> *God loves people so much that he gave his only Son so that whoever trusts him won't have to surely die but instead will have life to the full.*

Why did God not save Jesus, and why did Jesus not save himself? God was conspiring with himself to address the 'surely die' problem that has plagued us since the human race made its first wrong choice. He himself was doing the *surely dying*, for love's sake.

Contrast

If ever the 'tree of the knowledge of good and evil' was on display, surely that gibbet was it. The tree: a post with a crossbar; a tree with branches. But 'the knowledge of good and evil'? Well, 'the knowledge of good' was obvious: for Jesus to refrain from fighting back when he had the power to do so—but more than that, for him to actually love the so-and-so's who are abusing him to death—yes, that would give you the knowledge of what good looks like, good at its very best.

And 'the knowledge of evil'? All the ugliness of human abuse of free choice, nailing a good man to a pole and deriving entertainment from watching him bleeding, choking, suffocating to death. Good for you, human race! You sure know how to display evil in shocking colour.

'The knowledge of good and evil.' The ultimate contrast.

Ten Violations

As I read through the account of the execution in the Bible, I counted all ten of the Ten Words violated.

#10. Don't covet. They coveted his power and popularity, so it was envy that drove them to nail him there.

#9. Don't bear false witness. False witnesses working for the prosecution lied about him under oath at his trial. Perhaps even more serious, the judge and jury conspired to disbelieve him when Jesus told them the sworn truth.

#8. Don't steal. The executioners stole the shirt off his back after gambling to see who would win the right to take it home.

#7. Don't cheat on your spouse. Betrayed by a deceptive kiss! Jesus never was married, but it was one of his inner circle, one of his closest friends who cheated on him.

#6. Don't kill. Well, they sure disposed of that one, right?

#5. Honour your father and mother. They dishonoured both of Jesus' parents. God, as the father, was made to look uncaring, and Jesus' old mother, Mary, was totally sidelined as she stood beside her dying son at the foot of his gibbet.

#4. Don't work on the seventh day. A couple of other criminals who were sharing Jesus' fate were being too slow about dying, meaning the executioners would have to hang around after quitting time—and it was the weekend. Couldn't compromise their precious day off now, could they? So, they took a two-by-four to the shins of their victims to hasten the process, and they would have given Jesus the same treatment had not Jesus died before they could get to him.

Strange way to honour the seventh day as holy!

#3. Don't dishonour God's name. It was the religious people who were supposed to be representing a loving God who killed him. Who in their right mind would believe a word they said about love?

#2. Don't worship man-made stuff. The priests put Jesus down because they saw him as a threat to the stuff they worshipped—the bling of their precious religion, their temple, their traditions, their hierarchy, etc.

#1. Love God most of all. Love him? Never! They hated him to death!

Yes, the representatives of us, the evil old human race, ticked every box. Ten out of ten. God had sent us his most eloquent message to say: 'I love you!' And we humans replied in the clearest possible terms: 'But we hate you!'

Last Words

It must be hard to talk when you are suffocating to death, hanging from your wrists nailed to a plank. But Jesus did manage to choke out a few words near the end: 'Father, forgive them!'

If the Father could forgive the murder of his son, then surely he could forgive any sin. If he could forgive the mob who nailed his son to that cross, then perhaps he could forgive me. If Jesus was God's message to the human race to say 'I love you', well, 'Father, forgive them!' was the bottom line. It was like he said, 'I love you and nothing you could ever do will ever stop me loving you.' *Love never fails*. End of!

Finally, Jesus let go one last shout: 'It is finished!' Mission accomplished! 'Surely die'—all done!

Humans had abused God's gift of free choice to the absolute max. And the ultimate consequences had been given and received. God the Son had *surely died*.

Jesus had delivered God's 'I love you'. Message delivered in full. Jesus dead.

Morning After

But perhaps that's the problem. Jesus was dead. He's not much use to me or anyone else if he's dead, right?

And another thing… If that's the end of the story, we have to conclude that hate must be stronger than love; evil stronger than good; death stronger than life; man's 'No' stronger than God's 'Yes'.

If that's the end of the story, we are in deep you-know-what.

There's no clue given in the story as to how his buddies were feeling the morning after, but I'm guessing they were wrecked. They had followed him around for years, witnessed his amazing accomplishments, jotted down some of his wise sayings, been convinced that he really was God, pinned all their hopes on him… But now he was dead. All their great expectations down the toilet. They had been mistaken.

Back to the drawing board.

And for me too, that puts a big rusty nail in the coffin of my hopes and aspirations.

That is, if the story ends there…

Continuing Story

If I have followed the Bible's account accurately, the execution happened on the Friday morning. Jesus was dead and laid out on a slab in a tomb, sealed in by a big rock on the Friday evening. The religious folks feared body snatchers might make off with his corpse, so they set guards. All was quiet on the Saturday. Day off. But in the wee small hours of Sunday morning, while it was still dark, there was an earthquake that shifted the rock. The tomb was open—a big black hole to the regions beyond. The guards freaked out and ran off, scared spitless.

An hour or so later, just after sunup, a group of women arrived at the cemetery to do the honours, to embalm Jesus, or whatever they did to dead people in those days. They were worried about how they'd get past that big rock, so they were relieved to find someone had moved it. In they went. Nobody home!

A couple of glow-in-the-dark strangers told them Jesus was no longer dead but alive again, so it was no good looking for him in a cemetery. The girls ran off to tell the guys, but, understandably, no one believed a word of it. Nevertheless a couple of the lads ran back to the cemetery to check it out, just in case. They found things exactly as the girls had described: the rock shifted, the body gone, the sheet it had been wrapped in still there, but not tossed aside like someone getting out of bed, just sunk down like a deflated mummy.

Gobsmacked!

No one knew what to make of it, least of all the religious guys responsible for killing him. When the cemetery guards got back to the office, they were clearly shaken. Their suggestion that an angel must have rolled back the rock was obviously nonsense, but the guards clearly believed it. It took a pile of hush money to shut their mouths and to persuade them to circulate a story that during the night Jesus' followers had made off with the corpse. Funny that. Wouldn't the guards have faced serious repercussions for dereliction of duty? It must have been a hefty bribe!

But one way or another, that tomb must have been empty. The body must have disappeared. Otherwise, wouldn't they have just produced it and hung it up for all to see, thereby scotching resurrection stories?

So, where was it?

Things got worse over the next few days when Jesus' gang, the accused body snatchers, started blatantly announcing that Jesus was alive and that they had seen him—on one occasion five hundred of them all together at one sitting. A hallucination? What, five hundred people all seeing the same ghost all at once? Get real.

'Give them fanatics a few nights behind bars,' reasoned the religious brass. 'A little turn of the screw, the odd execution and they'll soon be singing from a different hymnbook.' But no. Not one of them caved. They all stuck to their story, till their dying days, as history would later show.

Anyway, back to that first Sunday…

Ghost

As the day wore on, the gang began to break up. Two of them left town and headed for home—time to get back to work rather than continuing to chase dreams. They fell into step with a stranger. I imagine they were so depressed that they never got their chins off their chests, let alone gave their travelling companion a straight look. So, it wasn't until late afternoon, when they all were sitting around the table to share supper, that they recognised him. Probably it was the obvious wounds on his hands from recent crucifixion that gave the game away.

Jesus! But then he was gone. Poof! They ran back into town to tell the others, only to find that some of them had similar stories.

While they were all sitting around the table, eating some fish sandwiches, in he came—Jesus.

'Peace!' he said.

Peace? Scared the you-know-what out of them. Thought he was a ghost.

So then he went through the old five-sense routine again. *Listen*. 'Recognise my voice?' *Look* at me. 'Remember my face?' *Feel*. 'Here, shake my hand! Touch me! I'm not a spirit.' *Smell*. 'Hey! Do I smell cooking? *Taste*. Are those fish sandwiches? Pass them up. I'm starving.' Ghosts don't eat fish!

Perfect communication. Conclusion. Jesus was alive.

Doubter

One of the lads wasn't there when this happened. He didn't believe a word of it the next day when they told him. Now, I'm with that doubting Thomas. That's me. I don't convince easy. Especially when it's something that I would love to be true but probably isn't. Wishful thinking can be a dangerous thing, right?

So, what am I thinking now, today, as I read the account in the Bible? Do I want all this to be true? Well, of course I do. If Jesus did come back to life after being dead for the weekend, it makes all the difference in the world. There's real hope, not just for me, but for my family, for everyone. So, all the more reason to be careful not to foolishly rush in where canny angels might fear to tread. If I so badly want this to be true, then I could well be in danger of fooling myself into believing something that isn't.

It was a whole week before Jesus showed up the second time. This time Thomas was there. 'Here, Tommy. Take a good look at this,' Jesus said, showing him the gashes in his hands where the nails had gone through. 'Seeing's believing, eh, Tom? Well, most people won't have the opportunity to see what you are now seeing, but their faith will come simply from words, by hearing about it from others. So stop your doubting and believe!'

'Jesus. My Lord and my God!' Tom said, dropping to his knees. Finally, what had started as a spark of hope hidden in his heart flared up into an open confession of Jesus as his Lord. The truth now in his own words.

Embryo

I think that's how it was for me too. At first, it was just a wish, a whim, a vague longing. I was fed up with the status quo and wanted something new. Then, I think, it was all that good stuff I had been reading in the Bible that hinted to me that something new might actually be possible.

Gradually, that secret longing grew into a hope: *wouldn't it be great if…* The more these thoughts have developed, the more my hopes have morphed into conviction: *yes, it really is true!*

It was like a new baby had been conceived in my heart—just an embryonic *wish* at first, a longing that matured into an inner *faith*. And eventually the baby was born, came out into the open as I put it into words. I verbalised my inner conviction and I said it out loud, just as Thomas did: 'Jesus, my Lord and my God.'

I was present when each of my three kids was born. Ugly little pink things they were. First thing they did was to let out a yell. Then we knew they were alive. One of them was a little slow off the mark, so the doctor gave him a slap on the rump. That did the trick. He's been yelling ever since!

Seems faith is a bit like that. Sooner or later it has to come out in the open and the first thing it does is give tongue, says something. I'm a little slow, so I admit it took a wee slap on my rump to get me talking, but eventually I let the secret out. I said it; I put it into words. I admitted that I now believe in Jesus. There was something about that simple acknowledgement that gave my new faith diplomatic status. I was out of the closet. Just like Thomas.

But unlike Thomas, my faith didn't come by seeing

anything. Obviously my five senses aren't much use 2,000 years after the event. There are no eyewitnesses left—the people who were there have been dead for centuries. The whole thing is literally ancient history.

I never was much for history, but I read a quote from one historian, a history prof at Oxford University in the UK, on the topic of Jesus:

> *I have been used for many years to study the histories of other times, and to examine and weigh the evidence of those who have written about them, and I know of no one fact in the history of mankind which is proved by better and fuller evidence of every sort, than the great sign which God has given us that Christ died and rose again from the dead.*

So, from a historical perspective, I don't have to be a complete fool to believe in Jesus' resurrection.

Beyond Reasonable Doubt

And then there was a lecture I attended by Norman Anderson, a professor of law. He said a lot of clever stuff about Jesus' resurrection; in fact, he wrote a book about it. But I remember his quoting a former Lord Chief Justice:

> *There exists such overwhelming evidence, positive and negative, factual and circumstantial, that no intelligent jury in the world could fail to bring in a verdict that the resurrection story is true.*

So who am I to argue?

I am old enough to vividly remember the Watergate scandal. Chuck Colson has always been vilified as Nixon's dirty tricks man. He was a smart lawyer, and the first one to be convicted of Watergate-related charges. So he knew something about lies and deception and had plenty of time behind bars to think it all over. Here's what he had to say about Jesus' resurrection:

> *I know the resurrection is a fact, and Watergate proved it to me. How? Because 12 men testified they had seen Jesus raised from the dead, then they proclaimed that truth for 40 years, never once denying it. Every one was beaten, tortured, stoned and put in prison. They would not have endured that if it weren't true. Watergate embroiled 12 of the most powerful men in the world, and they couldn't keep a lie for three weeks. You're telling me 12 apostles could keep a lie for 40 years? Absolutely impossible.'*

True

OK, so to believe that Jesus came to life again as reported in the Bible is not just wishful thinking. It's not true just because I want it to be true. It's true because it is true. And it's OK for me to want to believe. No need to hesitate for fear of swallowing a lie, since it is no lie. The truth is the truth, and I believe it. So now it's my turn to pass it on, which explains why I am writing all this down.

This is how one of the authors of the Bible put it:

> *What I heard I passed on to you: that Christ died for our sins, was buried, was raised on the third day, and appeared to Peter, and then to all twelve disciples. After that, he appeared to more than five hundred people at the same time, most of whom are still alive, though some have since died.*

Family Table

There's a famous painting of Jesus and his gang sitting down one side of a long table, posing for the photograph, I imagine. But surely the point of a table is that you sit *around* it, looking at each other, eye contact, friendly. I read in *Reader's Digest* that the table is the friendliest place in the home.

The Bible records that Jesus spent a lot of time chatting around the table with friends. That's nice; much more relational than sitting in rows like we do in the theatre or in church.

Anyway, there they all were, sitting around the table again when Jesus came calling after his big ordeal. I imagine him settling down with a mug of beer or a glass of wine or perhaps a nice cup of tea. From reading the account in the Bible and adding a little imaginative colour, just as Leonardo did, this is how I picture the conversation going…

Once all the questions had been asked and everyone had congratulated him on his miraculous recovery, he leaned forward and gave them the bad news.

'I'm not going to be with you for very long.'

'Where you going, then?' they asked, stunned.

'Going back to my Father.'

'Well, before you go, how about you introduce us? We'd love to meet him.'

'Don't you get it, even after I've been with you these past years? Here, shake my hand. Consider yourself introduced! I and the Father are one and the same. To meet me is to meet him. To see me is to see him. But don't think for a moment that when I say "I'm leaving" I am going to desert you altogether. Yes, I'm going to leave you, as you see me now—me in my human skin—but I'll be right back, me in *your* human skin.'

Well, that baffled them.

'The Holy Spirit! That's who I'm talking about. Just as I'm one and the same as the Father, so I'm one and the same as the Holy Spirit. One-in-three. Three-in-one. A trinity.'

Well, I doubt they did get it, so he continued. 'It is actually for your best that I vacate this mortal coil, since now I can only be in one place at a time. But when I return as the Spirit I won't just be *with* you, I'll be *in* you, all of you, all the time. I'll be in you like a hand in a glove, doing stuff through you, speaking through you, loving through you.'

Family Hug

They were still struggling to get his meaning when he put his arms round them and drew them all into a big family hug. He took a deep breath, then breathed out all over them. 'Breathe in. Breathe deep,' he said. 'My breath, my life — in you. Me in you. *Us* in you; me and the Father— both of us in you. Our Spirit in you.'

That was probably the moment when that insignificant gang of ordinary guys was transformed into a fearless fighting force that would make an impact on the world, the reverberations of which are still being felt to this day.

But Jesus wasn't done explaining important stuff… 'You will have noticed that I always address God as "Father". Well, that's because he is. He is my Father, and I am his Son. But now that my Spirit lives in you—the Spirit of the Son—you can call him "Father" just like I do. We are family, you see, one family.'

Family. So that's the plan! It's not a shiny new religion, better than all the others, more fodder for holy wars and arguments. And the plan has nothing to do with building institutions or organisations with rules for membership and articles of association. It's not even a twelve-step programme to empower people towards self-improvement. No. It's family. Us and God. Him a *trinity* and us joining together in twos and threes. *Family*.

I don't get the impression that Jesus ever intended us to make a religion out of it. I think he simply wanted us to be family.

I like that—me, part of the family, calling God 'Father'. A lot of people I know address him as 'Creator' or 'Higher Power', or just plain old 'God'. I suppose that's all fine as far as it goes—a good start. But *Father*! That takes things to a whole new level; that means that the relationship is personal, intimate, loving.

But back to what Jesus told them...

Family Business

'There's much to be done, guys, a world to save. Don't worry about the cost. I'll take care of it. You can charge whatever you want to my account. All you have to do is ask in my name. Just say: "Jesus said to charge it to his account." Actually, our Father himself is always tuned in when you pray. You don't have to ask me to ask him. No! He loves you, like I love you. Ask him yourself! He'll be tickled pink just to have you ask.'

'Love!' he says. 'That's what's important. It all starts and ends with love. So love each other, just like I have loved you. And don't be selfish about it. Don't try to keep it all as one little love-in, one holy huddle. There's a whole world of hurt people out there and they need to experience genuine love at street level so they can be drawn in. But don't just sit there expecting people to beat a path to your door. Go out and get them! You'll find them all around you, in your neighbourhood, your community, your hometown; all over the country; you might even have to cross oceans, since there are needy people as far away as the ends of the Earth. So go find them. Make friends with them. Draw them into the family circle. Tell them about me and all the things I have taught you about love.

'I am commissioning you as my ambassadors for peace and reconciliation. God is one and has always been in the business of reconciling people to be one with each other and with him. So now you, his children, have joined the family business: *peacemaking*.'

I get the impression that his brand of peacemaking was never about summit meetings of big-time political leaders discussing world peace. No, it was ordinary people coming together in twos or threes around the kitchen table. But isn't that the cornerstone of world peace?

Family Traditions

That was how it all started out. Those original followers of Jesus would regularly meet around the table. I guess they simply loved just being together, enjoying each other's company.

They would share a family meal—nothing fancy, just a loaf of bread and a glass of wine—but that always reminded them of Jesus, that he was still there with them, the host, the head of the table, even though they couldn't see him. So they'd drink a toast to him, imagining him sitting in his accustomed place, smiling at them all.

And they'd talk about him, recalling all the things he had said and done. Sermons and homilies? Possibly, but more likely just reminiscences of the good old days and what they needed to do in the here and now about all he'd taught them.

Then they'd read the Bible, maybe just a page or two. There they'd find promises of good things that God had in mind for them; stories of family heroes from days gone by; principles they might be smart to adopt; mistakes others had made that they would do well to avoid—all kinds of good stuff that must have precipitated many a lively discussion.

They would take time to encourage each other, particularly if someone was having a down day.

And they would pray. Not great long speeches; they just talked to God. What did they talk about? Well, what do friends and family ever talk about?

And how did they address him? Must have been a little awkward at first, him now being invisible. 'Father', since Jesus had told them that was what they could now call God. 'Our Father…' But sometimes they forgot and just called him 'Jesus', imagining him still sitting there in his favourite chair. But no one was too fussy, since to address the one was to address the other.

If someone could hold a tune or had a musical instrument, they might have had a family singalong, even stealing words from the Bible to save their writing original lyrics.

But they made a point of always having a few empty chairs. They never wanted to give the impression that the family circle was a closed circle. There was always room for more. And as soon as the meeting was done, they started right in, inviting new people to join them next time.

Family Initiation

And of course, it wasn't long before newcomers were wanting in and the original table just wasn't big enough any more. So they commandeered other tables around town and held multiple family circles. But they always stressed that they were just one family, and that newcomers were not joining a club, they were becoming members of the one family.

So the initiation into the family had to be significant. Signing on the dotted line or swearing verbal allegiance to Jesus just wouldn't cut it. No. Jesus had communicated his 'I love you' to each of their five senses, so the appropriate response of people joining the family needed to be a five sense 'I love you too' kind of event.

So what exactly happened?

They were dunked in a pool of water or a river. They felt it, saw it, heard it, smelled it, tasted it. At its most basic level, this dunking represented a bath, a washing away of the old messed-up life and the birth of a new beginning. Soap? Hardly, since it was all about spiritual cleansing and forgiveness, rather than germs. The Bible simply states that 'the blood of Jesus purifies from all sin'. It refers back to when Jesus was bleeding to death on the cross and he prayed for the people who had nailed him there: 'Father, forgive them.' So the water symbolised Jesus' dying prayer of forgiveness. *Forgiveness*. God's way of dispensing with the dirt of human sin.

But the significance went deeper than just washing. The going under was like a burial of the former life, a drowning. And the coming up again was like a resurrection, a new birth. The whole process echoed what Jesus had done. Down he went, dead and buried on Friday, then on Sunday morning, up he came. Resurrection! So the new family member identified with the ups and the downs of what Jesus had experienced.

And the newcomer would be welcomed into the family circle dripping wet, much like a newborn baby from his mother's womb.

I have attended a number of christening ceremonies in which the baby being welcomed into the family is sprinkled with water, a kind of pledge that there will be a subsequent baptism when the kid is old enough not to drown, mature enough to opt in for himself. The christening serves the dual purpose of also being a naming ceremony: 'I christen this baby Fred.' And it seems the original baptism served the same dual purpose. The new family member was officially renamed, given the right to the family name, the whole family that is, the trinity: 'In the name of God the Father, Jesus the Son and the Holy Spirit.' Well, how do you like that? A family celebration! Do I hear Champagne corks popping?

But this celebration was never to be confused with a graduation ceremony to honour something the new member might have achieved or extravagant promises he might have made. 'Not because of anything we have done', as the Bible emphasises, 'but to show God's love and grace to us.' Not so much an act of obedience as a peaceful expression of confidence that God will finish the job. I don't remember at any of those christening ceremonies any demands ever being made on the baby to have attained any passing grades to qualify to join the family, nor was he or she ever required to make any promises to undertake their share of the household chores or help pay the bills. No. It's just a welcoming event. No strings attached. I like that. A simple expression of trust in God to finish what he has started. Relax! Rest easy, like lying back in a hot bath after a long day!

Arguments have raged over the years about the precise manner in which baptism is to be performed. But that's not important. After all, it's only a symbol. It's not how it's done that is important, but who does the real baptising that counts. 'He, Jesus, will baptise you with the Holy Spirit and with fire.'

Family Circle

So here I am today, sitting at my kitchen table with a group of friends. The thing that makes me feel at home is the loving sense of togetherness we all feel around this table. Jesus said that love for each other would be the hallmark of his true family—the family likeness. So if that quality is not evident, I have to wonder if I'm in the right place!

The basic family circle still requires only a quorum of two or three. Jesus promised that whenever two or three people would meet together in his honour, he would join them. He, being a trinity, loves it when our togetherness in twos and threes mirrors who he is.

Sure, there are all kinds of family gatherings that happen in temples, cathedrals, churches and mosques, but I personally like the picture of a group of ordinary people gathered around the table. That's how it all started. Simple, basic, friendly.

There are meetings like that all over the world today, several in the town where I live.

The place of honour is reserved for the invisible presence of Jesus himself. There are always a few empty chairs, since newcomers are still welcome.

And now I'm one of them.

Yes, the family still is operational, still holding meetings along those same lines. Nothing much has changed. And there's still work to be done, a screwed-up world searching for that one thing.

I wonder what he's got in mind for us to do together today.

The Beginning…

CPSIA information can be obtained
at www.ICGtesting.com
Printed in the USA
FSHW010256311019